FROM
BLACK & WHITE
TO
CREATIVE COLOR

How to tone, tint, and retouch photographs

JERRY DAVIDSON

Pembroke Publishers Limited

© Copyright 1994 Jerry Davidson

All Rights Reserved. No part of this publication may be reproduced
or transmitted in any form or by any means, electronic or mechanical,
including photocopy, recording, or any information storage or
retrieval system, without permission in writing from the publisher.

Pembroke Publishers Limited
538 Hood Road
Markham, Ontario L3R 3K9

Canadian Cataloguing in Publication Data

Davidson, Jerry, 1935-
   From black & white to creative color : how to tone,
tint, and retouch photographs

2nd ed.
First ed. published under title: Light up your
darkroom.
ISBN 1-55138-025-0

1. Photography – Printing processes. – Toning.
2. Photography – Retouching. I. Title.
II. Title: Light up your darkroom.

TR335.D38 1994   771'.44   C94-930140-X

Cover Design: John Zehethofer
Cover Model: Shannon MacMaster
Typesetting: Jay Tee Graphics Ltd.

Printed and bound in Canada by
D.W. Friesen & Sons Ltd.

0 9 8 7 6 5 4 3 2 1

Contents

WITHDRAWN

To Shirley, with love.

Preface

Back in the early 1800s, when the technology of silver-based black-and-white photography was introduced, the chemist-photographers who pioneered in this field immediately began the task of discovering methods for producing full-color images on photographic plates. They experimented with gold, sepia, selenium, and blue toning, as well as with dye toners and hand coloring. Ultimately, dye chemistry, from its crude infancy, grew into full-color photography, which in its most rudimentary form is nothing more than toning of multiple layers.

The techniques and materials for colorization — the toning and hand coloring of black-and-white photographs — have been significantly updated; they now provide us with many opportunities for creativity. Magazines frequently use colorized images in ads to highlight fashions, cosmetics, or jewelry, and in articles to depict people and represent issues in an eye-catching manner that neither black-and-white nor full-color can command. Colorized images also appear on record album covers and hang in private and public art galleries, personal living rooms, hotel lobbies and office buildings. The powerful images created by these new techniques have captured the attention of and appeal to the tastes of people everywhere.

The material in this manual deals mainly with — though I hesitate to use the term — that "gray" area between the black-and-white print and the full-color photograph. We will primarily concern ourselves with an aspect of darkroom technique that has received little attention and about which little practical information exists; that is, the manipulation of the black-and-white print by the selective addition of color. You will also learn how to use materials and techniques to do corrective retouching (the price we sometimes pay for our mistakes), as well as more innovative retouching — a more advanced application of toning and tinting.

Although colorizing a black-and-white photo is a complex subject that can be approached in different ways, I hope to give you the basic information you will need to launch your own experiments and develop your skills. You won't find a lot of messy chemical formulations or technical mumbo jumbo. The procedures and techniques are straightforward; they require no special equipment or previous training and may all be carried out in the darkroom with the lights on!

Like the photochemists before you, you are limited only by your imagination. But unlike them, you can depend on proven methods and materials. Turn the page and turn your black-and-white prints into color.

Jerry Davidson
Salt Spring Island, B.C.

1

The Need To Colorize

BEFORE YOU BEGIN

This is a good time to consider what effects you might want to achieve by adding color to your black-and-white prints. We should agree at the outset that colorization by toning and hand coloring is of little value or meaning, except when it is thought of as a means of enhancing an image in some way. You may find some very practical reasons for wanting to add color to a black-and-white print. Suppose, for example, that you find yourself someday in the embarrassing position, as I did, of having come away from a shoot with a black-and-white image only to discover later that it should have been in color. In this instance hand coloring may be your only salvation. Consider this next tactic when you submit black-and-white contact sheets or proof prints to an art director. Tone them in a distinctive monotone color so that they will stand out in the pile of black-and-whites from your competition. An eye-catching ploy. Alternatively, you may have a black-and-white image or series of images that can be turned into beautiful art-quality photographs suitable for framing. With a little appropriate colorization, you can tastefully pick up key colors in such items as carpeting, furniture, or drapery to coordinate your photographs with the overall decorator scheme.

Whatever the reason, the general objective in any manipulation of a print should always be to enhance the beauty or presentability of the image, to alter or heighten its mood, or to increase its impact and graphic appeal.

For those of you who are interested in obtaining maximum permanence for your prints, a growing body of opinion suggests that an archivally processed print is not truly archival unless it has been protected in some manner. Toning is one way of achieving this. It can be done in different ways: by treating with a metallic type of toner, or by using Berg Selenium Toning Solution or Gold Protective Solution. I'll have more to say about this in chapter 7.

In other words, toning must result in a discernible benefit; it is very unlikely that simply toning or adding color to a bad photograph will somehow transform it into a good one.

We all know that our reaction to color is a subjective experience, and it would be presumptuous and reckless of me to dictate what sort of image modification you should attempt or what colors you should employ. I can only make a few general suggestions, give a few examples, and leave it to your good judgment or whim to take it from there.

You may find, for example, that just a slight addition of a cool or warm tone will provide you with a very subtle but nonetheless desirable effect. On the other hand, there may be times when you will want to abandon caution completely and lay strong color in selected areas for a bold and dramatic transformation of the print. Between these two extremes there will be an almost infinite scale of possibilities for you to explore. Please understand that the illustrations in this manual are only meant as a guide. I encourage you to unharness your own imagination and ingenuity, and experiment freely.

Remember that toning and hand coloring gives you an advantage over normal color photography in that you can be selective about where the color goes and you can control to some degree the intensity of each color.

For this book, I have chosen to use Berg Color-Tone Inc. products in my discussion and illustrations. This is quite intentional; I do not apologize for it, nor do I mean to suggest that by omitting to mention a competitive product that it could not be used. However, in my view, Berg has the most complete selection of toning, hand-coloring, and retouching chemicals and materials from which to choose, and besides being virtually odorless, their products are the most versatile and easiest to use.

For instance, the Berg line of toners, toning assist formulations, and retouching dyes work well with all silver-based emulsions including resin-coated (RC) and fiber-based (FB) papers, films, transparencies, and even emulsion images on other materials.

SOME TERMS DEFINED

Before we begin to discuss some of the specific methods and materials, we should first clarify the terms "toning" and "tinting". I will deal with each in more detail later.

Toning

Toning is the process whereby the silver particles, which are suspended in the gelatin layer and make up the various grays and blacks of a black-and-white image, are converted chemically into a colored form. In this case the paper support (backing) receives little or no color. Berg makes

a line of toners of this type, known as metallic toners, which both impart a distinctive color and protect the print at the same time. The formation of colored metallic salts results from the reaction of the toner with the silver particles. Often the color of the toning solution is quite different from that of the final toned image. Berg makes a selenium toner that is also effective in protecting the print but has only a limited effect on the color of most images.

Toning, then, can have more than one meaning. Occasionally in the text I will use the term toner, or toning, in the broadest sense, meaning any formulation that imparts color to a photograph by forming a colored metallic salt, or a dyed image, but most often I will be referring to a specific type of toner as described above.

Tinting

Tinting refers to the technique of partially or entirely staining the entire gelatin layer with colored dyes or other substance so that the paper support and the gelatin layer receive the color (the silver image in a tinted paper does not). In other words, in tinting the color penetrates the entire material, and, being dyes, the color of the dye solutions will, of course, match the tint which they impart to the print. Another major distinction between toning and tinting is that the dyes in tinted images can often be totally or nearly removed by prolonged washing.

There are ways, however, to localize the dye so that it "sticks" to only the silver image of tinted prints. The Berg Color-Toning System contains an Activator Solution, which provides the "glue" or mordant that holds the dyes tightly, so that they will bind to wherever there is a silver image. In this process, known as "mordanting", the silver image is first converted chemically into an almost colorless silver compound and on tinting with certain organic dyes, the dyes adhere to the silver compound. If the Activator Solution is not used, only tinting will occur on immersion of the image in the dye bath.

There are, of course, a number of other methods of adding color to a black-and-white photograph, and, although they aren't included in this manual, you should feel at liberty to try anything you wish, from dunking your print in beet juice or tea, to applying color with pencils or paints. I acknowledge that from the standpoint of the purist (one who would look on anything beyond simple protection of the fine art print as tantamount to heresy), the degree of print manipulation I am going to discuss will often seem severe. I make no apology for this. Although RC papers don't rank high on anyone's list for so-called fine art printing, it is hard to discount their unparalleled versatility for commercial and nonarchival applications. Many of the effects we will produce will be striking, daring, even outlandish, and while we might join in applauding the skill and devotion of the fine art printer, we also recognize that many equally dedicated amateur and professional photographers welcome new, exciting, and, yes, commercial effects to add to their inventory of darkroom knowledge.

SOME BASIC CONSIDERATIONS

A Word of Caution and the Need for Good Housekeeping

Any chemical formulation handled carelessly can be harmful, and, although the majority of photographic products are generally safe to use, sensible precautions should always be considered an essential part of darkroom technique. Read the instructions and any cautionary information of any photographic formulation carefully. Some persons are particularly sensitive to photographic chemicals; to avoid needless skin irritation, they should always use tongs, and in some cases wear rubber or vinyl gloves. Some formulations should only be used with suitable eye protection (safety glasses). Always work in a well-ventilated area, even outdoors on a nice day. Keep all formulations out of the reach of children! Similarly, never allow any chemical to contact the eyes or mouth. Never, for instance, wet a retouching brush with the tongue. Before you start, read carefully all of the precautions and remedial

actions that come with each product. Good housekeeping is just a matter of sound and sensible caution and plain old common sense. Wash up as you proceed: trays, tongs, gloves, and any spills.

Print Preparation

Proper print preparation will have a significant effect on the final toning result and I will remind you occasionally of this factor when discussing the procedures that follow. In order to achieve predictable results it is extremely important that you always use *fresh* developer and fixers when processing your prints, and adhere to the wash times recommended for the various processing and toning formulations.

Spotting and Retouching

It is usually best to leave any minor spotting and retouching until after the toning or tinting has been carried out so that you will be better able to match the final color and blend in any corrections. Basic retouching technique is dealt with in chapter 5.

Fixers

A special caution is needed with regard to the type of fixer you use. Under normal circumstances, avoid the use of hardening fixers, which, as you might expect, cause the emulsion to harden and then act as a barrier to toners and may even prevent toning. Remember: *fresh, nonhardening fixer*. As well, do not overfix but adhere to the minimum times for fixing as recommended by the manufacturer. A nonhardening fixer may be prepared from Kodak Rapid Fix by not adding the small bottle of hardener to the formulation. Alternatively, if a print or film has already been hardened, Berg manufactures Dehardening Solution to reverse the hardening process.

Washing-Aids: Berg Bath™

You should heed a word of warning when it comes to the use of washing-aids in the processing chain. Most washing-aids do the job for which they are designed; that is, they are effective in removing the thiosulfate (hypo) that can be detrimental to print permanence and which may interfere with proper toning if not washed out. However, what is not commonly understood is that washing-aids do not necessarily remove themselves easily and this can cause toning problems. Not so with Berg Bath™, which washes out easily. My general advice is that for resin-coated papers, which normally require a short washing time, you can be satisfied with a normal one-fix cycle followed by a thorough wash. With fiber-based papers, however, I recommend Berg Bath™ and a simple wash cycle before toning.

If you still have problems with uneven toning or staining of highlights and borders, then the problem may be in one or more of the following areas: the particular photographic paper you are using; hardening of the emulsion caused by excessive washing after fixing in hard water; inadequate washing after toning; if a bleaching or activation step is required, insufficient washout of bleach or activator; or toning under fluorescent lighting. A little experimentation with several photographic papers will usually reward you with a better choice. Excessive washing in hard water can harden an emulsion, even though you carefully used a nonhardening fixer. Berg Dehardener Solution will wash out that hardening and minimize or eliminate highlight staining. Also, Berg Bath™ turns out to be an excellent standby for washing toning, bleaching, or activator chemistry out of prints. Finally, toning under incandescent lighting will decrease staining while increasing the useful life of the toning bath.

A word of warning in washing toned prints: excessive washing after Brilliant Blue or Golden Yellow toning can cause loss of tone and image, depending on your water quality. Again, Berg Bath™ comes to the rescue by hastening washout of the toning chemistry and shortening the final wash time. For machine-washed prints, include an extra wash step to avoid contamination from dirty rollers or incomplete washing.

Other Emulsions

Berg toners are effective on all types of photographic emulsions including the various makes of resin-coated and fiber-based papers, films, transparencies, and even emulsions on other materials such as fabrics or metals. Toning times will vary between one paper or film product and another, with slightly different results (warm paper versus cold paper, for instance). You should always make a test strip first and keep some record of your results for later reference. Remember that the intensity of toning will depend largely on the following factors: the concentration of the stock solution, the age and depletion of the chemistry, the type of material to be toned, the temperature of the solution (the warmer the faster), and, finally and most important, the length of time in solution. Moreover, whether you are toning or tinting or just applying a touch of color, there is ever present what I would term the "unpredictability factor". Sometimes your results will be just plain baffling, though not necessarily undesirable.

Dilution and Amount of Toner Solution

We would all like to economize as much as possible on our chemicals and materials, and for this reason you might be tempted to dilute the solutions beyond the normal stock concentration recommended, in order to stretch them. Fair enough, but you will have to accept the fact that you may not get the results as predicted by the manufacturer and will therefore have to experiment on your own.

As a guide, use enough toner solution in your trays to adequately cover the size of print you are working with in the same fashion you judge the amount of developer or fixer to use.

Hardware and Cleaning

Whenever possible use plastic trays and tongs when toning rather than stainless steel or enamel because of the danger of discoloration and spotting caused by traces of rust. If you like to keep your trays in pristine condition then line them first with plastic wrap before pouring in the toner

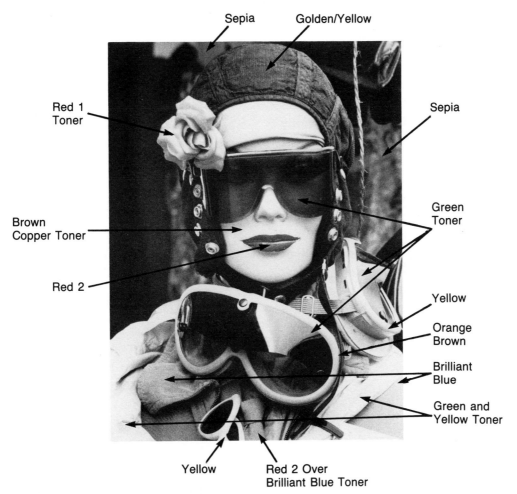

Sepia

Golden/Yellow

Red 1 Toner

Sepia

Brown Copper Toner

Green Toner

Red 2

Yellow

Orange Brown

Brilliant Blue

Green and Yellow Toner

Yellow

Red 2 Over Brilliant Blue Toner

This shot of a mannequin in a flea market in Amsterdam was enhanced with the addition of eleven different colors from the Berg line of products, using various techniques. Some colors were applied with a sable brush; others by masking out certain areas of the print and then either swabbing on the color with a brush or cotton ball, or immersing the entire print in a toner bath. Each method and color is discussed in this manual.

solution; otherwise wash them out with soap and water immediately after toning, or soak them in a 1:1 solution of household bleach and water.

Similarly, store your stock solutions in glass or plastic bottles out of room light. With many toning solutions, after they have been standing for some time, a scummy sediment may form in the bottom of the container. When you prepare to tone or tint, carefully pour the solution into a tray leaving the sediment behind (decant), as you would a fine wine to avoid contamination. As a further precaution you can decant through a paper filter (coffee filters are excellent). Wash out your stock bottle and get rid of the sediment before pouring the stock solution back into the bottle. Formation of sediment does not mean that the toner is exhausted; it could well last for another few months.

Agitation

When toning either prints or films it is important to keep fresh toner in contact with the emulsion. For prints, intermittent agitation is usually sufficient; however, in the case of film, continuous agitation is important and a processing drum is often useful. During toning or tinting, keep prints separated, and make sure the film strip does not double back on itself so that the surfaces touch.

TO SUM UP: THE BARE BONES OF COLORIZING

Reduced to the simplest possible terms, toning or tinting is a matter of mixing up some chemicals according to directions, pouring the solution into a tray, immersing a print for a given amount of time, and following up with a wash to stop the process and remove unwanted residue. But wait! Before you go rushing off to the darkroom, please take a few moments to review the basic considerations that I have just covered; they will save you unnecessary disappointment later on.

I will deal specifically with each type of Berg toner in succeeding chapters, but here is an outline of the main points:

1. First read the manufacturer's instructions carefully, especially safety information.

2. Prepare your print using fresh chemicals.

3. Avoid the use of hardening fixers. Some toners will give colored solarization if prints are hardened. Other toners may not tone at all. Use Berg Dehardener Solution to soften hardened prints.

4. Berg Bath™ is a unique, environmentally safe hypo eliminator that is also effective as a washing aid after toning, bleaching, or activation.

5. Before attempting to colorize your print, make a test strip and record the data with regard to time, dilution, etc. (See the data sheets in chapter 9.)

6. Use sufficient toner in the tray to adequately cover the print and agitate intermittently.

7. When things still go badly, go back and read the instructions again.

2

Metallic Toners

WHAT THEY WILL DO FOR YOU

Remember in the first chapter I discussed some of the essential differences between toning and tinting, notably that the so-called metallic toners convert the silver particles in the image to a colored form? As you will see, the effects are often quite striking and unique. We are now ready to tone our first print and will begin by using one of the Berg metallic toners to transform a black-and-white print (either FB or RC papers) into a uniformly monocolored print. At the same time remember you will be imparting a protective element to the print that wasn't there before.

The Five Metallic Toners

Berg manufactures five metallic salt toners: Brown/Copper, Brilliant Blue, Golden/Yellow, Selenium, and RC Sepia. Each toner is distinctive in terms of the color and depth of tone that it imparts to the print, but all five share some common properties, which I will outline here. With the exception of the RC Sepia, which requires a two-bath process, they are single-bath toners and all can be used in normal room light. Also, none of the toners has an offensive odor, and all, except for Selenium, are "forgivable", which means that they can usually be reversed back to the original black-and-white image, either totally or partially by redevelopment. But a word of caution: refixing a toned image is usually unnecessary and, in some instances, can be detrimental, especially if followed by redevelopment.

Toning Procedure

I'll begin by outlining the general procedure to be followed when using any of these toners, and then include specific commentary and examples of each type.

1. Pour enough of the toner solution into your tray to adequately cover the print.

2. Prewet the print.

3. Slide the print into the solution and begin timing immediately. Agitate intermittently.

4. In just a few seconds, you should begin to notice that toning is beginning to take effect. At any time remove the print from the solution, rinse it in a water bath, and examine it under a strong light before returning it to the tray of solution, or you may stop the toning process altogether by washing. As a general rule, wash for at least the same amount of time as you would after fixing. (You can also hasten the wash process after toning by placing the toned print in a solution of diluted Berg Bath™ for three minutes; then wash thoroughly.)

5. When you are satisfied with the degree of toning and the print has been washed as directed, hang it up to dry or, less preferably, place it in a print dryer. If you use a print dryer, set the temperature at a low level to prevent degradation of the colors.

Toned 30 seconds.

Toned 2 minutes.   Toned 5 minutes.   Toned 30 minutes.

I especially like the Berg Brown/Copper toner for its versatility and its broad range of chromatic effects depending on the time you leave it in solution. With short immersion times it is particularly useful for imparting a warm flesh tone to portraits and figure studies. On the other hand, if the print is left in the toner bath for an extended period, say thirty minutes, the hue that the toner imparts to the print will intensify dramatically. Results will vary with the type of photo paper.

In the series of five photos of the body builder, you can readily see the effects of prolonging the immersion time and the different results that can be obtained. The range of tones in this case extends from a slight warming of the print after thirty seconds in the toner (top, right), to a rich, reddish copper color after thirty minutes in the toner (bottom, right), with variations in between.

Be aware that as the toning intensity increases while the print is in the toner, another effect becomes

evident that is peculiar to just this toner. Brown/Copper has a tendency to "open up the shadows," so that as the toning progresses through the various stages, the deeper blacks in the shadow areas of the print begin to lighten and reveal detail. For this reason, when you plan to tone a print for the richest possible effect, your original print should be overexposed by at least 50 percent to produce a deeper density. This may require some experimentation and is helped by using a test strip.

This characteristic of the Brown/Copper toner can be seen readily in the final print, which has been given twice the normal exposure. The result is a very dark print. However, notice how prolonged toning caused the shadows to open up and the contrast to soften. Remember to allow for this characteristic of the Brown/Copper toner when toning for extended periods.

This print was made on Ilford Multigrade FB (fiber-based) paper.

14

Toned 30 seconds.

Brilliant Blue toning solution is the most vivid and dynamic of the Berg metallic toners. It has a full range of tones depending on the toning time, from an initial slight cooling effect, to a pastel blue, through to a final vibrant tone that would approximate an ultramarine blue found on an artist's palette.

The toner works quickly. The final effect will depend on the immersion time and the type of material to be toned. Brilliant Blue also has a tendency to intensify the image, and for this reason you might consider preparing a lighter than normal print, especially if you are going to prolong the toning.

Again, a test strip is the best way to guarantee results.

For prints, this toner works particularly well with "cold" images such as glass, snow, water, sky, shiny metal, or any object that calls for a cool or moody appearance.

The print shown above was made on Ilford Multigrade II paper and toned in a stock solution of toner for thirty seconds. I have also had good results with this toner, and somewhat better control, when the stock solution is diluted 1:1 or even 1:2 with water.

Image Reversal by Redevelopment

I have already alluded to the fact that you can often completely reverse the effects of the Berg metallic toners. This is done by redeveloping the image in a dilute developer (your old print developer diluted 1:5). After redevelopment (that could take anywhere from one to ten minutes), and when all the toning has been removed, rinse the print in an acid stop bath, wash well, and dry. You are back where you started ready to retone if you wish. (Note that in the case of RC Sepia toner this procedure is slightly different. See the note with the figures on page 23). In these days of escalating costs this is a particularly helpful procedure because it allows you to experiment freely and often salvage what might otherwise be a botched job.

This redevelopment procedure can also produce some unusual and unexpected results. During redevelopment in a highly diluted developer (say, Kodak Dektol 1:20), the reversal process is slowed down and the image goes through some interesting stages, which consist of grays, blacks, mid-tones, and a "solarized look" (meaning the light to dark tones in the image appear to be reversed). This special effect is described in detail in the next section.

COMBINING THE METALLIC TONERS FOR SPECIAL EFFECTS

As a general rule, any of these toners can be used in combination for some unique and striking effects. To do this you must deviate slightly from the usual procedure and introduce an additional factor into the toning procedure. Incidentally, the term "solarization" for our discussion is not a true solarization, but a similar effect whereby the print tones reverse themselves to some degree, seemingly from positive to negative. Also, when I refer to "posterization", an effect where the continuous tones of a normal photographic image are separated into tonal blocks, I am referring to an approximation of this look, not a true posterization technique.

I warned you earlier about the hazards of using a hardening fixer when preparing your prints, because of a barrier set up by the hardener that inhibits toning. We'll now turn this around and use hardening to our artistic advantage.

Develop a print as you would normally, only this time use a hardening type of fixer such as Kodak Rapid Fix, or add a small amount of hardener to your regular fixer (the amount may have to be established by experiment, but as a starting point use about one half the amount recommended by the manufacturer). Fix and wash the print as before, but do not overfix.

If you tone your print in the Brown/Copper toner solution, for instance, you may notice a posterization effect taking place. That is, the deep blacks will tend to stay dark for some time, the middle grays will accept the toner and take on a bright copper tone and the lightest grays will bleach out. Some of the tones may even appear to have reversed themselves, that is, become solarized. If all this sounds vague and uncertain it is meant to be. The fact is, results will be unpredictable and will vary with the type of paper, the image, and the toning and redevelopment times, all part of the unique appeal. This time, using the same redevelopment procedure as before, redevelop the image partially in a very weak developer, say Dektol 1:20, just to the point where the lightest grays begin to return. At this point quickly return the print to an acid stop bath for a few seconds and then wash again. You now have a partially toned print with most of the color in the middle to dark areas, and possibly some beautiful posterization/solarization effects.

The next step is to add a second color to the lighter areas only, by any method of your choice. You can, for example, take a cotton swab or brush, saturate it with Brilliant Blue toner, and selectively lay on the solution to those areas where you want to produce a cool contrasting color. Alternatively, you can immerse the entire print in a bath of Brilliant Blue toner. Watch the process carefully until you have reached the desired level of secondary toning. In either case, when the level of toning is where you want it, remove the print and place it in a water bath for a thorough wash. In this same fashion you can add additional colors to make up a multi-toned image. Later I will show you how to combine the metallic toners with some of the organic dye tinting colors.

You can experiment with this technique using any of the metallic toners in any order, but because Brilliant Blue is such a dominant color it is best to use it in the second phase.

TONING FILM

Although toning film perhaps doesn't strictly qualify under the title of this book, it is worth pointing out here that some toners can also be used to tint film for viewing as a positive transparency. Brilliant Blue is one of these toners and I'll briefly describe its special use.

The color blue, incidentally, has been found to be the most pleasing and restful color for viewing. White lettering, charts, and graphs on a bright blue background can be easily and inexpensively produced, and will provide you with slides ideally suited to educational, scientific, or home entertainment presentations.

Just about any black-and-white negative film can be used provided that the density of the blacks does not have a "Dmax" value greater than about 2.5. ("Dmax" means the maximum density of silver, and is therefore the blackest part of the image.) Litho films have very dense blacks, which do not tone suitably, and for this reason I recommend, in addition to the toner, a roll of fine grain, medium to high contrast panchromatic film (Kodak AHU microfilm 5460), which is ideally suited to this work. It has a Dmax value of about 2.2 and an ISO rating of about 6; it can be conveniently processed in Kodak Dektol or Kodak D-19 developer giving crisp, professional results.

Using the Film
The work that you intend to copy should ideally be line copy, that is, crisp black lines or lettering on a white background. You can use a combination of pen and ink or rub-on lettering for this purpose. Set the material to be copied on a flat surface or copy stand, and be sure that your camera lens is absolutely perpendicular to the subject plane. Even lighting is also essential; a pair of photoflood lamps of the same wattage at a 45° angle to the work plane will serve adequately. Use a gray card held over the work to take an exposure reading, and on your first roll bracket the exposure, and record the results for future reference.

Processing and Toning the Film
Here is the basic procedure for completing the processing and toning operation; more detailed instructions are contained in the package and should be followed carefully.

1. First load the film into a plastic tank (the toner will stain stainless steel tanks) and give the film a pre-wash.
2. Develop the film in Kodak Dektol or D-19 for the time and at the dilution recommended.
3. After development give the film a few seconds in a stop bath.
4. Wash the film.
5. Now tone the film in a freshly made stock solution of Brilliant Blue toner for eight minutes with periodic agitation.
6. Wash again.
7. Fix in a hardening fixer.
8. Finally, wash for the third and last time.

When the process is complete you have a diazo-like blue transparency that is silverless and very stable in color. The Golden/Yellow toner can also be used for toning film, as can some of the organic dyes discussed in chapter 3. Instructions for their use in toning films come with the packaging.

Selenium Toning Combined With Other Toners
The benefits of Selenium toning for archival purposes is discussed fully in chapter 7; however, it

The print shown above was made on Ilford Gallery paper, toned for five minutes in Berg Brown/Copper toner, washed and then redeveloped for 45 seconds in a dilute (1:15) solution of Kodak Dektol until some of the lighter grays from the original image began to reappear and the image took on a slightly poster-ized look. At this point the print was given a rinse in an acid stop bath and washed.

Next I placed the print on a flat surface in my sink, and with a large soft brush began to swab Brilliant Blue toner stock solution onto portions of the win-dows and floor in the image. The Brilliant Blue toner was only allowed to stand for about one minute before the print was given a final thorough wash.

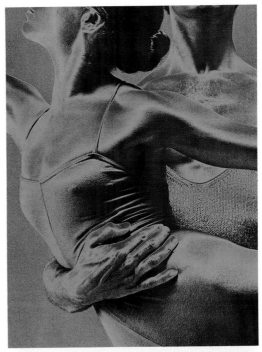

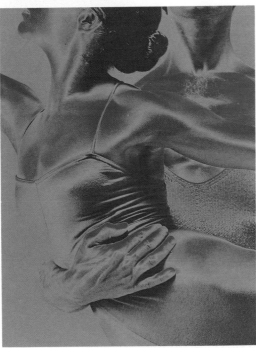

After I printed this promotional shot for a ballet company I was impressed by the fact that the figures looked almost like a piece of metal sculpture. To enhance this look I made an actual solarized print by switching on the overhead light for about one second while the print was approximately one-third of the way through development in the tray. Then I completed the development. I used Ilford Multigrade paper and a high contrast filter to make a harder image.

One print (top, right) was toned in Brown/Copper toner for eight minutes (I had overexposed the print by approximately 75 percent to allow for the shadows to open up). A second normally exposed print (bottom, left) was toned in Golden/Yellow toner for five minutes. A final print (bottom, right) was made by soaking a print in Brilliant Blue toner for two minutes and, after a brief rinse, transferring the print to a bath of Golden/Yellow toner for an additional three minutes. The result was a deep, rich green quite unlike anything I had seen before.

19

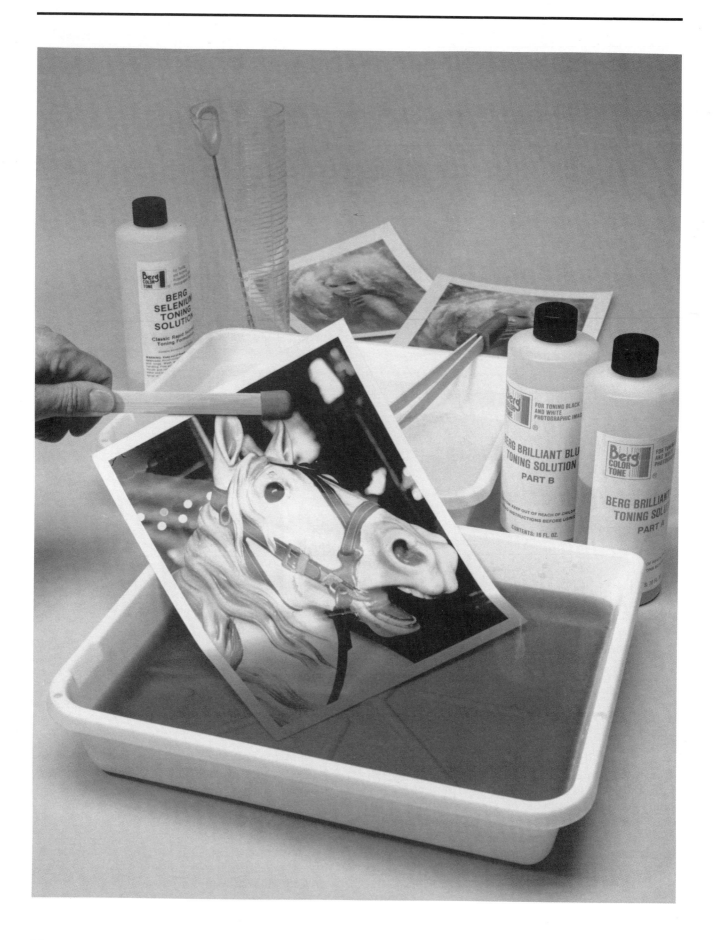

is worth mentioning here that you can achieve unique color combinations by combining Selenium toner with any of the metallic toners.

Toning a print with Selenium usually results in a shift to a significantly warmer tone in the image, especially if using a warm-toned type paper or a bromide type paper. (Technically speaking, the more silver contained in the paper emulsion the more pronounced the toning effects. RC papers don't respond well.) This effect can be used to even greater advantage when coupled with the already described tonal changes brought about with Brown/Copper, Brilliant Blue, or Golden Yellow toners. In my experience, a more pronounced duotone effect can be gained by using Brilliant Blue in combination with Selenium toner; however, you may find some surprising and appealing results when you use any of the metallic toners in this fashion.

I would recommend the following as a general procedure, but, as usual, don't hesitate to experiment freely on your own. Prepare your print in the normal manner and give it a five-minute soak in Berg Bath™ with intermittent agitation prior to the final wash. Next, immerse your print in one of the metallic toners until you see clear signs of a shift in tonal color, especially in the darker areas. Now immediately switch the print without washing into a bath of diluted Selenium toner (1:10 or greater dilution to start with). As a rule, you will soon see a distinctive warming in the lighter areas of the print; this is the time to transfer the print quickly to a water bath to arrest any further changes to the tonal development. Finish off with another full wash cycle. The timing for each stage of this progressive technique cannot be predicted exactly, and the results will vary from very subtle to a distinctive duotone combination.

Toned 1 minute.

Toned 1 minute; refixed
20 seconds.

Berg Golden/Yellow toning solution is a metallic toner that will progressively tone an image to a rich golden-yellow color over a period of about ten minutes. On its own it is effective in imparting an eye-catching graphic appeal to prints, or it can be combined with any of the other toners for unique results.

If, after toning a print in this solution, you should refix the image, the final image will be a bright yellow, but it will be silverless. This explains why you cannot use the redevelopment technique to reverse an image that has been refixed because the image may be lost altogether! This particular toner is also sensitive to fluorescent light, and you should tone your prints under a weak incandescent light.

I took this shot on a blistering hot late summer day in the Japanese countryside. When I made the print, however, it just did not convey the right feeling. I gave the first print a bath in Golden/Yellow toner for about one minute, but the result was a bit too golden. I toned a second print in the same manner, then I refixed it for twenty seconds. This time the print had a slightly bleached and more dazzling yellow look to it, more in keeping with the original scene as I remembered it.

Printed on Ilford Multigrade II paper.

RC Sepia toner.

Brown/Copper toner.
Toned 5 minutes.

Berg Rapid RC Sepia toning solution is a 'true'' sepia toner, which imparts a warm yellow-brown look to prints (in comparison the Brown/Copper toner tends towards a reddish brown), and is just the thing for that old-fashioned appearance in a restored photograph or wherever a warm tone would be appropriate.

Unlike the other metallic toners, this toner is unique in that it is a *two-bath* process. The two solutions are prepared and stored separately; the first, a bleach bath, and the second, a toning bath. There is no ferricyanide in this toning bath as you find in other sepia toners and, remarkably, it has none of the rotten egg smell usually associated with sepia toners. Also, unlike the other toners, which vary in intensity depending on the time in solution, this toner will usually produce a single tone for a given paper. However, if the sepia tone is too dark for your needs, dilute the toner bath 1:1 or 1:2 with water for lighter shades of sepia.

Don't be horrified when, after immersing your print in the first bleach bath, your image begins to disappear. Leave the print in the bleach bath for approximately one to two minutes or until only a ghost of the original image remains, following which the print should be washed (RC papers for three minutes, FB papers for five to ten minutes). Dilute Berg Bath™ will hasten washout of the bleach chemistry. Next, place the bleached and washed print into the second tone bath until the image is thoroughly sepia toned (anywhere from one to three minutes). Finally, wash the toned print thoroughly.

The old worn boots hanging on the wall on a fishermen's net shed seemed to be the perfect type of subject to illustrate the effects of sepia toning. The print was made on Ilford Multigrade II paper. Although the toner has been especially formulated to work well with RC papers, it is equally effective with all FB papers.

3

Tinting and Toning With Organic Dyes

ORGANIC DYES VS. METALLIC TONERS

Not to be confused with any of the metallic toners, which constitute a system in themselves, organic dyes provide you with an alternative and even more versatile means of adding color to your prints. Although the results may be similar, the system is based on a completely different type of chemical reaction.

Berg makes a line of organic dyes that come in different sized kits under the name of the Color-Toning System. Remember that organic dyes penetrate the emulsion layer and affect not only the blacks and grays in the silver image, but tint the white portions of the paper support as well. For this reason I think of their application as tinting, if the activator step is eliminated.

A TWO-STEP TONING PROCESS

In the Berg Color-Toning System, dye-toning is a two-step process that requires an *activator stage* to provide the glue (mordant), which prepares the silver image to receive the colors, and a *tinting stage*, which is the actual application of the dyes. Both stages can be carried out in full room light. Depending on the kit you buy, you will have at your disposal a selection of water-soluble, concentrated dyes that can be mixed together to provide any combination of additional colors. The concentrates in the kit are diluted with water in proportions that are determined by the type of material to be tinted, that is, prints or films.

Once overall dyeing is accomplished, the highlights or white areas on the print can be cleared in a final step so that the color is left bound to only the silver image, or, if you prefer, the entire print can be left in a toned and tinted condition.

The Procedure

I will now outline in some detail the techniques for toning or tinting prints with organic dyes from the Berg Color-Toning System.

1. Prepare your print in the normal manner observing the same precautions that you did for toning with the metallic toners. That is, always use fresh developer and fixer, and to guarantee consistent results, avoid the use of a hardening fixer. Use Berg Dehardener Solution if the print has been prehardened or washed excessively in hard water. Adhere to the manufacturer's recommendations for washing after fixing.

2. Mix the Activator and the concentrates in the kit in accordance with the instructions, and note that the dilution for film is different than that for paper. Pour enough of each solution into separate trays to adequately

cover the print. Make up a third tray of the Clearing Solution.

3. Tone an exposure test strip first to different toning intensities and record the data for future reference.

4. Immerse the print in the Activator Solution with intermittent agitation for anywhere from three to ten minutes depending on the intensity of the tone required (the longer, the deeper the tone that will be imparted). The image will turn a brownish gray during this stage and should be washed thoroughly to remove all traces of excess Activator, which, if not eliminated, can inhibit proper clearing of the highlights in the later steps. Diluted Berg Bath™ will rapidly and effectively remove residual activator formulation from prints.

5. Next, place the print in the dye solution and begin gentle agitation again. Leave the print in this solution until you are satisfied with the degree of toning, a matter of about two to five minutes.

6. Finally, clear the highlights to the degree that you wish using the following procedures. It is possible to clear the highlights from any of the colors by simply submerging the print in still water for ten minutes to several hours. For the Red-1, Green and Violet, however, treat the print in the selective Clearing Solution until the highlights have cleared and then wash for two to fifteen minutes before drying. Another method of clearing is to use a solution of one to two ounces of glacial acetic acid (concentrated stop bath) to a quart of water. Immerse the print until clear. The last method, *if all else fails*, is to use a weak solution of ordinary household bleach, say,

one-third ounce of bleach to one quart of water. This last solution can also be used to remove the stains from trays.

Regardless of the method used to clear the highlights, you will find that the ease with which this is accomplished is largely dependent on the type of material and the color. Some colors, notably Yellow, Green, Blue-1, and Red-1, seem to wash out more readily than the others. Also, as you might expect, resin-coated papers and films wash out more easily than fiber-based papers.

Tinted Papers
By eliminating the Activator step you can produce your own tinted papers. Simply place the black-and-white print directly into the color bath until you're satisfied with the color intensity in the emulsion. Then wash out the excess color. Squeegee off water droplets and dry.

The Colors
A brief look at an artist's color wheel will give you a glance at some of the secondary and tertiary colors that result from mixing two or more hues. To get a more precise idea of what to expect when you blend the colors of the Berg Color-Toning System use an eyedropper or brush to combine two or more colors in a small cup or palette, and then test the resultant on an old photograph or a piece of white cardboard.

You can, if you wish, combine the effects of the metallic toners with any of the colors in the Color-Toning System, although bear in mind that the latter are not as forgivable as the metallic toners and cannot be reversed.

An Artist's Color Wheel

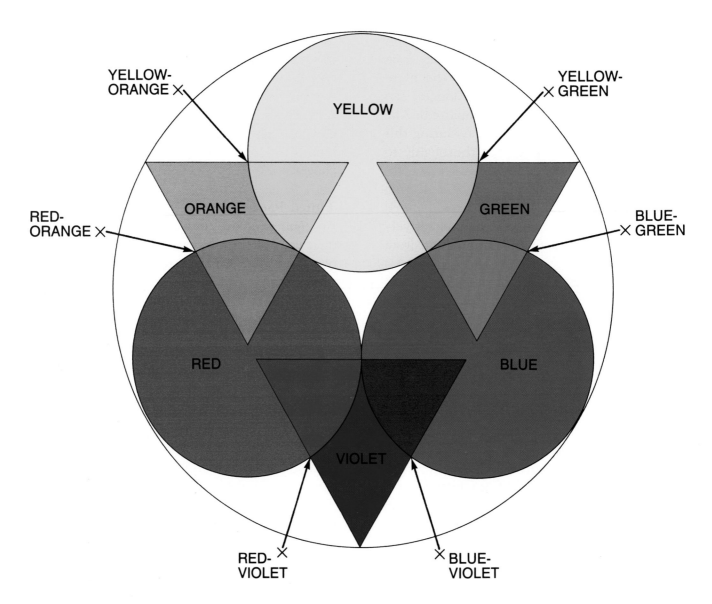

YELLOW-ORANGE ✕

YELLOW-GREEN ✕

YELLOW

RED-ORANGE ✕

ORANGE

GREEN

BLUE-GREEN ✕

RED

BLUE

VIOLET

RED-VIOLET ✕

✕ BLUE-VIOLET

○ PRIMARY COLORS

▽ SECONDARY COLORS

✕ INTERMEDIATE COLORS

I captured (you should forgive the pun) this "woodsy nymph" on infrared film and printed it on a grade 4 Ilford Multigrade II paper. The print was given an activator bath for five minutes, washed and then toned for five minutes in Green from the Color-Tone Kit, which I thought would enhance its spooky atmosphere. The highlights were cleared in a dilute solution of glacia acetic acid.

The costume for the model in this shot, incidentally, was made by an artist friend of mine, Bonnie Campbell.

4
Methods of Selective Toning

MASKING OUT

Although normal procedure calls for immersing the entire print in a tray of toning solution for an overall transformation, it is possible, and often desirable, to selectively tone only certain parts of the print. The technique employed to do this is called "masking" and involves blocking out those portions of the print that you do not wish to tone. There are different ways of going about this.

The Puddle Method

If you aren't overly concerned with crisp, well-defined borders between the toned and untoned areas on the print, the simplest method of toning is to lay the print flat in the sink or on an empty tray, and with a cotton swab or brush lay some toner in a puddle on just the area or areas to be toned. On a dry print, surface tension will hold the toner reasonably close to the area you wish to tone. Move the swab or brush around gently within the puddle of toner to provide a certain amount of agitation so that the toner can do its work. Toning times will of course be slower, because you are only using a limited amount of toner. If you are not getting results fast enough because the toner appears to be exhausted, rinse off the old toner, squeegee the surface, and apply fresh toner to the same area.

In this manner you will build up the toning effect in successive stages.

Liquid Masking

When the portion to be toned is relatively small in terms of the total print area, a single face, perhaps, or even a pair of eyes in a portrait, then use a liquid masking medium to contain or block out the toner. Masking fluid is often used by watercolor painters to mask small areas on the paper, and can be found at most art supply dealers under various brand names. The fluid has the look and consistency of thick cream and behaves in about the same fashion as would a diluted form of rubber cement, which, incidentally, can be used as a crude substitute. Apply the masking fluid with a brush (an old one is recommended); it dries quickly to a rubbery film, which is impervious to the toner and which you can easily peel away without any harm to the print emulsion. (The sticky side of masking tape removes it easily, or you can rub it off with your finger or a soft eraser). You can use this type of masking fluid either to form a dam of sorts to surround a small puddle of toner, or to cover a certain portion completely to protect it from the effects of the toner bath. In a pinch you can even use petroleum jelly in the same fashion, although it does not flow on as easily, and you must afterward remove it with a suitable household solvent followed by a thorough wash to remove any trace of solvent.

Frisket Paper Masking

There will be times when you will want to selectively block out relatively large areas on the print, and at the same time retain clearly defined borders between the toned and untoned portions. The material used in this case is called frisket paper and comes in sheets or rolls of thin transparent film, which is slightly adhesive on one side, fixed to a paper backing. A graphic arts store is probably your best source of supply, and although a similar type of material is made by various manufacturers, you should specify that you want the "low-tack" variety. The advantage of low-tack frisket paper will become apparent as I explain how it is used.

First, cut a piece of the frisket paper to a size slightly larger than the dimensions of your photograph. Now very carefully, with a sharp knife, slit the edge between the film and its paper backing and slowly peel away the film, holding it by one corner. Discard the paper backing. Align the film along the top edge of your photograph and slowly roll it down into place over the entire print surface smoothing it as you go with a cloth or piece of rolled tissue to eliminate any air bubbles trapped beneath.

The next step is a little tricky and you may find you require some practice on old prints before it is a completely successful operation. I use a swivel-bladed knife made by Ulano Company, which is specifically designed for this purpose, but you can easily get by with a fine-bladed knife or even a razor blade. With your knife, very delicately trace a line on the film around the contour of the area to be toned using just enough pressure to score the surface, being careful not to penetrate through to the print below. In fact you will find that there is really no pressure required; just the weight of your hand is probably sufficient to make the very shallow incision that is required. Now, with the tip of the blade (I use a duller blade for this operation), gently pry up one of the corners of your incised line,

and as the film starts to separate take the edge between your fingers and peel it away. It is here that you will appreciate the superiority of low-tack brand frisket film to other types; it allows you to separate the film cleanly and easily in the exact contour that you have cut. It is an action similar to separating one postage stamp out of the middle of a sheet by tearing along the dotted line.

You have now opened a window, in effect, and exposed a selected portion of the print surface for toning. Gently rub the cut edges of the window with a tissue to make sure they haven't lifted off the print. If you have done the operation properly you can slip the entire print into a bath of toner without fear that the toner will penetrate under the film. When toning is complete, peel the remaining film from the print, and discard. Wash the print according to the toning instructions.

You can, if you wish, repeat the masking and selective toning process almost any number of times for a multi-toned effect using any of the methods described. In practical terms, however, two or three separate tonings would be a sensible limit.

The facade of the building in this photo's background was very distracting and took the focus away from the central subject. Dodging out the background during printing was not a very practicable solution, so I decided to try some selective tinting with one of the colors from the Berg Color-Toning Kit.

First I made a "mask" with frisket paper blocking out the figure of the skateboarder, the wall, and the border areas. I then immersed the entire print in a bath of Red-1 for approximately ten minutes. (I chose Red-1 in this case to better illustrate my point.) I chose not to activate the print first because I wanted to tint the entire background, not just those portions that contained silver. The last step was to strip away the mask and give the print a final wash.

In chapter 5 I discuss various ways of masking.

I originally shot this photo in black-and-white for a program cover; it was later decided to go for a certain color combination. Here was a good opportunity to experiment with the airbrush and some of the colors from the Berg Color Retouching and Hand Coloring Kit.

First I masked out all of the subject area with low-tack frisket paper, and then immersed the entire print in a bath of Golden/Yellow toner for six minutes. Next I gave the print a good rinse and placed it in a second bath of Brilliant Blue toner until the combined colors gave me the right shade of green (about two minutes). Once the print had been washed and dried I set to work with masking paper, the airbrush and some colors from the Color Retouching and Hand Coloring Kit at full strength. Some of the smaller areas were hand colored with a sable brush.

31

5

Retouching Black-and-White Prints

SOME BASIC CONSIDERATIONS

This is a good time to look at the fundamentals of "corrective" retouching as applied to black-and-white prints, especially before we introduce some of the more freehand methods used in "innovative" hand coloring.

I don't make any claim that this will qualify as an in-depth study of the many facets of print correction and restoration. I will, however, give you some practical guidance and helpful tips on methods and materials used to eliminate minor flaws and correct imperfections, problems common to all of us. These simple techniques will also serve as an important adjunct to the procedures you will develop in other areas of print enhancement described in this book. In short, the aim is to broaden your knowledge and range of skills so that you will be able to tackle just about any area of print manipulation with confidence.

Contrary to what you may believe, basic print retouching is neither full of mystery, nor fraught with great technical difficulty. It does, however, require that you exercise a certain amount of patience, and, as is the case with most things worth doing, that you practice in order to gain proficiency.

An Ounce of Prevention

The most effective means you have of reducing the amount of time and labor spent retouching is the care and attention you give your negative before it goes into the carrier of your enlarger. I don't suggest that you go through a surgical scrub each time you enter the darkroom, but with a little attention to a few simple practices, you can prevent most problems.

Housekeeping

Eliminating dust entirely from the darkroom is a difficult and often futile task, but you would be surprised at just how effective an occasional clean-up with a mop and sponge can be. As a personal rule I regularly damp-mop the floor of the darkroom and take a slightly damp sponge to the counter tops, workspace and around the enlarger. The component parts of the enlarger itself are also cleaned frequently. Incidentally, when it comes to vacuum cleaners, the exhaust port probably negates any benefit gained by the suction port, and for this reason I never use one in the darkroom.

I should also mention that my cameras also get regular attention, since one of the most common problems is grit or dust on the film pressure plate. Dust can leave a scratch on the film as it moves across. I use a soft cleaning brush and an airspray can to keep out these offenders.

Storing the Negative

Proper storage of precious negatives is essential, not only from the standpoint of dust, but also to protect them from scratches, abrasions, and the effects of pollutants. Keep them filed separately in glassine envelopes, which you can purchase at any photo supplier, and when you remove them be sure to handle them by the edges only. Oils from the skin can be damaging over time. If you should get a fingerprint on the negative, remove it by gently applying a negative cleaning solution with tissue, also available at your photo supplier.

Cleaning the Negative

Detecting a tiny dust particle or bit of cat hair on the surface of the negative requires more than just a cursory glance. To do it properly hold the strip of film by the edges and examine it under strong light at an oblique angle, turning it back and forth slightly to reflect the light and illuminate the culprits. A gentle puff of breath might be just enough to dislodge whatever is there, but a better and safer method is to use an air bulb combined with a soft sable brush. Finally, a careful wipe with an antistatic cloth is the best insurance that any particles will not only come away cleanly, but will not be attracted back again. Remember that the whole purpose of this procedure is to somehow lift the dust or lint off without damaging the vulnerable emulsion surface. That is precisely why wiping the negative is the last step. This minimizes the danger of dragging a piece of grit across the surface of the film.

Treating Scratches on the Negative

There are a number of ways to handle the problem of a lightly scratched negative. In each case the purpose is to try to fill in the scratch with a clear medium that has the same refractive index as the film material; not an easy task. One of the oldest tricks in the book, and probably one of the most effective, is to take your finger and rub along the side of your nose picking up a coating of skin oil. Now very gently and delicately, with a circular motion, apply a very thin film of oil to the scratched area. (Don't worry, it will be removed later.) In the same fashion you can apply a small amount of petroleum jelly or baby oil, but be sure that it is applied very lightly, and that you remove it completely afterward with a soft tissue or cloth. A third alternative is to use a commercial product such as Edwal No-Scratch, which is applied with a small brush or cotton ball. In my experience nothing but the mildest scratch seems to respond favorably to any of these treatments, and none of the above methods can be used in conjunction with a glass negative carrier. Keep in mind that very light scratches on either side of the film will print as light lines, while a scratch that is deep enough to penetrate right through the emulsion will result in a black line on the print, and will have to be handled in a different fashion. I will discuss this problem under print retouching technique.

You may have wondered about the possibilities of making corrections directly to the negative, and although I don't eliminate this as a possible course of action it is outside our scope to discuss it here. It is generally impractical to work on a 35mm negative, which is the format favored by the majority of people, and negative retouching does require some specialized equipment and training.

Common Problems

Print spotting, then, is the term used to describe the most common and frustrating task you will have to face. This is the process of eliminating small defects on the print caused by scratches or dust particles on the negative. The goal of print spotting is that it should be absolutely unobtrusive, particularly if the print is an "exhibition" print to be displayed in the gallery, home or office. On the other hand, there are times when more radical correction or retouching is done to a print that is to be reproduced in, say, a magazine.

TOOLS AND MATERIALS

I will only deal with the basics of print retouching and will not burden you with the concern and cost of acquiring a large collection of elaborate tools and materials. I'll give you, instead, the essentials to get you started. As you become more efficient and courageous, expand your equipment stock as you see fit.

The most important requirement will be a suitable workspace. In a pinch, the kitchen table will do, a slant-board is better, and an adjustable drafting table would be the top choice. Regardless of your selected working area, however, it is more imperative that you have proper lighting in the form of some sort of movable lamp head that can be brought down close to the work.

Retouching Pencils

These are the basic retoucher's tools and probably the most useful ones for making minor corrections. Retouching pencils, favored by many retouchers, come under various trade names and are made especially for marking on paper, glass, plastic, metal, and, in our case, glossy prints. They come in assorted colors, but for our purposes the ones to start with are those that look like an ordinary lead pencil but which work well on a glossy surface. They can be found at most photo suppliers or graphic arts stores. For working on matte surface prints, which will be discussed under spotting technique, you will also need a selection of ordinary lead pencils.

Brushes

Retouching brushes are also important items and this is one area where it is definitely not wise to economize. A good red sable brush such as those sold by Berg as part of their Touchrite Brush Kit will last a long time if looked after properly and will allow you to do your best work. Brushes come numbered by size starting with No. 0000 (the finest) through to about a No. 3 (the thickest for practical retouching purposes). Some top retouchers use what we would regard as a fairly thick brush even for very fine work. They will tell you that a good quality brush should be able to hold an extremely fine point regardless of the size, and that the large number of hairs in a thicker brush will hold the dye much like the action of a fountain pen, even though the tip remains almost dry. It is likely, however, that you would be satisfied with either a No. 00 or No. 2 for most purposes.

Color Palette

This is usually a small metal or plastic tray with shallow depressions for holding different retouching colors. You can probably get by with something improvised, such as a plastic egg tray or ice-cube tray, but a proper one is a handy thing to have. It comes as part of the Berg Touchrite Brush Kit, or can be purchased at any artists' supplier.

Etching Knife

The etching knife is nothing more than a very sharp-bladed tool used to pick or scratch away tiny dark spots on the print surface usually in preparation for adding a lighter tone. A graphic arts knife with a pointed blade is an economical choice or you can simply snap off a razor blade at an oblique angle. Resin-coated papers do not respond well to etching with a knife; restrict this operation to fiber-based papers.

Cotton Gloves

Oil from the skin can damage a print or inhibit the flow of retouching dyes. You should wear cotton gloves when retouching. Most photo stores carry them; they are not expensive and are certainly a good investment. If you feel that wearing gloves is a hindrance, try cutting off the thumb and first two fingers on the glove of your working hand to make it easier to hold the brush. At the very least you should always lay tissue or tracing paper under the heel of your hand to protect the print's surface while you work.

Magnifiers

Your local craft store will likely carry a type of magnifier favored by hobbiests who work with finely detailed equipment. It might be on the

This was an attempt to restore an old and badly damaged snapshot culled from the family album. I set up a makeshift copy stand and, with a macro lens and fine-grain film, photographed the snap through a piece of plate glass to keep the print flat. After enlarging the copy print to an 8″ × 10″ size, I examined it carefully to see what retouching would be required and what approach I should take.

The main problem was to eliminate as much of the damaged area as possible on the right side of the print. A secondary consideration would be to remove some of the background clutter, and increase the overall contrast and sharpness of the detail on the figure. First I made an oval mask from a piece of cardboard, and on the second print I dodged out a lot of the extraneous background keeping the figure central. Next I set to work with a fairly wide brush and a squeegee, and with successive applications of ferricyanide (see page 39), I progressively bleached away most of the damaged area. I then decided to enhance the old-fashioned appearance of the print by toning it for about five minutes in a stock solution of the Brown/Copper toner. (I could also have used RC Sepia.) After the print had been washed and squeegeed almost dry I did some extensive brush retouching using a combination of organic dyes from the Berg Color Retouching and Hand Coloring Kit and the Touchrite Kit. Some of the other colors were applied in dilute form using a cotton swab or large brush.

expensive side, but it does have the advantage that it fits over the eyes from a head strap and frees both hands for working. However, I have found that if you secure your work to the slant table or work on a flat surface you can easily get by with the standard "Sherlock Holmes" magnifying glass, which you can hold in your free hand.

Other Helpful Items

I have listed the basic tools you will need to begin, but as you become more confident you might want to add other materials to assist you in the job. Felt-tipped or fiber-tipped pens are sometimes helpful in spotting out small white areas on a dark background. An ink eraser that comes wrapped in paper like a china marker is useful for abrading a small area of a print to give it a little "tooth" so that the retouching fluid will penetrate more readily. It seems inevitable, as with any hobby, you will acquire additional paraphernalia: cotton swabs, cotton balls, tissue, eyedroppers, and just about any variety of jar or bottle that strikes your fancy and you feel you can't live without.

BASIC PRINT SPOTTING TECHNIQUE

Now that we have organized our workspace and assembled our materials, let's select a suitable sample print and get down to the business of learning and practicing the technique of print spotting.

Printing paper, as you know, comes in a variety of surface textures ranging from a hard gloss to a softer matte texture, and in different shades from a so-called cold tone to a warmer brownish or sepia tone, depending on the manufacturer. Whether you use retouching pencils or spotting dyes you may have to experiment by combining one or more mediums to match the exact paper tone. Test your mixture on a separate practice print before working on the final print.

Working With a Retouching Pencil

At the easiest end of a scale you might have one or two small white dots to deal with on an otherwise perfect print. If the spot is small enough and

on a middle gray background you might easily remove it by touching the spot with the sharp tip of a retouching pencil using a vertical downward pecking motion. With matte surface prints there are also times when just an ordinary lead pencil can be used for good results. Fine white lines or spots in an area of very delicate gray tones can be handled with the use of a hard lead pencil such as 3H or 5H. Fuzzy or blurred edges in a light toned area can be made more crisp in the same fashion. If your pencil line is too sharp try softening it with a gentle rub of the finger or a cotton swab.

With a very delicate touch and a little practice you can also become adept at applying graduated areas of shading using the flat of the pencil lead, blending it further with a cotton swab. This has a very soft effect similar to the results you get from "burning in" an area of the print under the enlarger. Similarly, you might try using the graphite dust that comes off an ordinary soft pencil lead (a 2B for instance) when rubbed on fine sandpaper. Again, use a cotton swab or ball to blend in the powder over the area to be corrected. Finish off the print with a light spray of clear photo lacquer or apply a small amount of steam from a kettle to soften the gelatin surface slightly and thereby "fix" the graphite dust onto the print.

Brush Work and Retouching Dyes

If the pencil or felt-tipped pen won't do the job, then your next step is probably a brush and retouching dye.

Retouching dyes are designed specifically for print spotting and correcting and can be purchased in liquid or cake form. Applied most often with a brush, but sometimes with a cotton swab, dyes (diluted with water) penetrate into the emulsion to become part of the print. Retouching dyes do not penetrate a glossy surface as readily as they will the more absorbant matte surface and you may find it necessary, on a glossy print, to add a drop of a wetting-agent such as Kodak's Photo-flo to the dye before you attempt retouching. A little saliva works in much the same way, although you should never develop the habit of

This print of a tray of fish in a Honolulu fish market was colorized with a combination of a metallic toner and a selection of colors from the Berg Color Retouching Kit. My intention was to treat the image in a soft-edged manner using muted colors in the tradition of a watercolor painting. To begin, I gave the entire print a short 30-second bath in Brilliant Blue toner to impart a hint of silver-blue tone to the fish scales and followed up with a wash. Then I began to work on the still damp print with a soft hair brush using very dilute colors from the Color Retouching Kit, gradually building up the color tones in blended layers. The final accents in the eyes and body stripes were added with the colors straight from the bottle.

dabbing your brush on your tongue after taking up some dye on the brush. Instead, use the back of your thumbnail or the edge of the palette cup to wipe any excess from your brush tip. In more desperate situations an ink eraser, if used gently on a small area, will impart a tooth to the paper finish and help the dye to penetrate. Severe corrections may look too obvious, and will have to be covered up with a glossy clear lacquer spray that you can buy in an aerosol can from a photo supplier.

You can also buy opaque "retouching grays", which come in tubes and range from near white to black, to be diluted with water as needed. Opaques do not penetrate like dyes, but sit up on the print surface. For this reason, when they are used for retouching, the print is usually recopied or reproduced in some other form such as in a newspaper or magazine. There are other opaque mediums that can be used with varying amounts of success such as watercolors, oils, various types of inks and even acrylic paint.

The Berg Touchrite Kit contains a selection of concentrated dyes ranging from neutral black to gray to warm black and white (a non-penetrating opaque medium). In addition, Berg offers a Color Retouching and Hand Coloring Kit containing a full line of colored dye concentrates that can be used for color print retouching, or for adding selected areas of color (hand coloring) to a black-and-white, color, or toned print. Just about any intermediate shade can be produced by blending and diluting the dyes with water.

When applying retouching dye, never try to match the final tone the first time, instead, work with diluted mixtures so that by successive applications you gradually work up from light to dark to the final density. Allow each layer of retouching dye to dry and then examine the result carefully before applying the next.

Remember that dyes do penetrate and are generally permanent. You can, however, reverse the effect somewhat by soaking the print in water or by blotting the spot with a cotton ball dipped in a solution of one part household ammonia to ten parts water.

Technique

Your brush should contain only a small amount of fluid at the tip. Grasp the brush firmly between the thumb and first two fingers, and hold it in a near vertical position over the area to be touched. Now, as you did with the pencil, apply just the very tip of the brush in a delicate pecking motion to the defect. The idea is to blend a series of dots together into a single tone. If you are working on a hair line, begin at one end of the line and progressively spot your way down the line, turning the print if necessary. Try to let the hairs of the brush tip contain the dye within the borders of the line as if you are filling a trench without touching the sides. This takes some practice, and you shouldn't be discouraged if you find on your first few attempts that you spill over the edges. Stick with it; perfection will come.

Color Print Retouching

Although it falls outside the scope of this book, you should know that many of the procedures and techniques that we have outlined in making corrections to a black-and-white print also apply, to some extent, to color prints, or to prints that have already been toned. However, the more complex the color combinations become, the more demanding your retouching task. A certain amount of trial and error may be necessary in order to accurately match color tones and densities.

Berg's Color Retouching and Hand Coloring Kit provides you with a full spectrum of color dyes for just about any corrective or creative retouching purpose. The ten concentrated transparent colors come in handy one-ounce bottles along with a plastic palette and a set of two fine red sable Berg Touchrite brushes. The dyes are formulated to be diluted with water, and can be blended to any desired combination.

The technique of color print spotting is carried out in the same manner as with black-and-white retouching. Dilute the selected color with water in the palette provided, and apply the dye with just the brush tip, allowing each layer to dry before adding more. Examine the print carefully at each step.

Keep some old discarded prints on which to practice before committing yourself to any final work on your print. Another alternative is to lay a piece of thin acetate over the print and do your experimenting with color hues and densities on the acetate before tackling the print.

Treating Black Spots and Lines

Pinholes or deep scratches on the negative, as I've said, will print as black marks during the enlarging process. It is often possible to treat the smallest of these marks in one of two ways: either apply a minute covering amount of retouching white or, in the case of fiber-based papers, with an etching knife very gingerly abrade the surface mark revealing the lighter tone underneath. In both of these cases, however, there will be some evidence of the correction, a situation that you may not find acceptable, especially if you intend to exhibit your print. The alternative is to first reduce, or bleach, the offending mark chemically to a lighter or white tone, and then retouch back to the proper tone with either a pencil or dye as you would with any other white mark. This process, called chemical reduction, is described in the next section.

Chemical Reduction

Potassium ferricyanide is a yellow crystalline powder that, when mixed in solution with water and a second chemical, sodium thiosulfate (sometimes called "hypo", the main constituent of fixer), becomes known as "Farmer's Reducer". Kodak sells both chemicals separately, available in jars, or in a packet labelled Farmer's Reducer. All you really need to buy, however, is the potassium ferricyanide (the active ingredient), a jar of which will last you for years. I know photographers who use their own modifications of this basic technique, but here are some easy and effective methods of employing this useful chemical to eliminate or reduce dark spots, or lighten dark areas of the print.

First let's deal with the treatment of isolated black spots on the print. To begin, very slightly moisten the area on the print with water and squeegee it almost dry. Then, with a barely damp brush, pick up a single orange crystal of the potassium ferricyanide on the tip, and at the same time be prepared with a cotton ball soaked in ordinary print fixer (a simple substitute for sodium thiosulfate), and have a ready supply of running water nearby. Set the yellow crystal directly onto the black spot to be bleached out, and watch for just a few seconds as the crystal begins to absorb some of the moisture from beneath. Now quickly apply a generous amount of fixer with the cotton ball and follow immediately with a rinse of running water. The fixer acts as a catalyst and completes the bleaching action. Squeegee the print and examine the results. If necessary repeat the applications in the same sequence until the spot has been eliminated completely or reduced sufficiently. Finally, after refixing the print, give it a thorough wash, allow it to dry, and then apply pencil or retouching dye in the normal manner until you have matched the surrounding tone once again. There is some tendency to overcorrect on your first few tries, but you will soon learn when to stop the action of the ferricyanide bleach.

For bleaching out dark lines or larger dark spots on the print, or for simply lightening certain areas (the white of the eye, for instance) it is best to work with the potassium ferricyanide in solution. To do this, shake a few grains of the potassium ferricyanide into a cup, add a couple of ounces of water and stir the mixture until all the crystals are in solution. The exact solution strength is not critical but is arrived at by experimentation. As a starting point you should look for a light yellow color, and if this proves to be too strong you can always add more water. Try out your dilution on some old prints first to get the feel of it and then dilute more if necessary.

Lay your print on the back of a tray or piece of glass that is slanted towards vertical in your sink, apply the working solution to the print with a brush and allow it to stand for only a few seconds before hosing with water. You should notice a slight lightening effect, and there will be a faint yellow staining around the worked area. Next, immediately immerse the print in your tray of fixer, and watch to see that all traces of yellow stain vanish and the bleaching action is completed. Check the results and reapply if necessary until the desired reduction is achieved. When you are satisfied with the result, refix and wash the print again as you would at the end of any processing sequence. Finish off by retouching the bleached area with a pencil or retouching dye as necessary. Don't be tempted to use a strong solution; you will likely over-correct.

The Airbrush as a Retouching Tool

You have no doubt heard of the miracles wrought by master retouchers using an airbrush. This versatile device, which is nothing more than a miniature spray gun, is indeed capable of producing amazing effects in the hands of an expert. Airbrushes, however, are expensive, require additional ancillary equipment (which is also expensive), and must be kept scrupulously clean and in top working order. Skill in using an airbrush can be acquired, but long hours of practice and some training are necessary before one becomes truly proficient. Nevertheless, airbrush courses are often available through art schools and continuing education classes, and this is a good way to learn the basics and decide if you want to invest in your own airbrush. Most retouching dyes on the market can be used in an airbrush.

The choice of color-print film for this country churchyard in bright sunlight turned out to be inappropriate for the mood I intended for the subject. On a whim I took the color negative and simply printed it on a fairly high contrast black-and-white RC paper. The eerie blue-on-purple duotone effect was created using the following procedure. First, the print was immersed in Activator solution from the Berg Color-Toning System for five minutes. Next, the print was placed in a one-quart bath of a mixture of 1:1 Blue-1 and Red-1 from the Color-Toning System for about two minutes. I then placed the print in an acid stop bath until the dark tones turned a deep purple and the highlights took on a lighter blue tone (about ten minutes). Finally, after the print had been washed and dried, I covered the entire print with frisket paper, incised and removed the film covering the church, and, with a brush and a very dilute solution of household bleach, progressively removed the blue tone from the face of the church until it appeared to glow. The print was given a final wash. Happily, the result had just the sort of surreal effect that had eluded me in the beginning.

6

Hand Coloring Black-and-White Prints

Many years ago, before the advent of color-print films and papers, it was common practice for photographers to hand color (or hand tint, if you prefer) their black-and-white prints. Today, interest in this old technique has been resurging, except that now we have the advantage of newer and better formulations and a much greater range of methods and materials from which to choose. Let's take a look at some of the usual ways to approach this innovative area of print enhancement.

To begin with, the only limiting factor when it comes to manipulating a black-and-white print is how far you are willing to extend the leash on your imagination and creativity. Archival permanence aside and discounting any misgivings you might have about altering the pristine quality of a silver-based image, virtually any colorant that can be applied to the surface of the print is fair game.

Most photographers and artists (in this area it's difficult to distinguish between them) prefer the time-honored method of tinting the black-and-white image with artists' oil-based paints. Oil paints come in a wide assortment of colors and can easily be applied with a brush, cotton swab, or the tip of a finger for a soft, muted effect either straight from the tube or diluted with a suitable solvent such as turpentine. Similarly, water-based

paints such as watercolors or acrylic colors, or even colored inks and felt markers, can also be used with effective results.

Remember, on the one hand, that these sorts of colorants do not completely penetrate to become part of the emulsion; hence they will produce a more "painterly" result. Vegetable dyes and certain inks, on the other hand, although they do penetrate the surface, may prove to be far less permanent and far more prone to fading compared with formulations intended specifically for photo retouching.

FREEHAND COLORING WITH DYES

A suitable alternative to artists' pigments are formulations created specifically for use with photographic silver-based emulsions. The organic dyes in the Berg Color Retouching Kit are well suited for hand coloring black-and-white prints to produce effects similar to those obtained with oils or watercolors. Both RC and fibre-based papers accept these dyes readily, but you will obtain the most uniform results on a matte-finish fibre-based paper.

For a soft, pastel-like result, you should work with a slightly damp print (dunk it and then wipe it with a squeegee), and the colors should be

Of all the metallic toners, Brilliant Blue is often my first choice for an overall background tone, especially when I plan to superimpose other colors. The elements of this image demanded a hard-edged treatment, so I began by covering the entire print with frisket film and with a swivel knife removed the background areas leaving the tulips and stems covered. The print was immersed in a bath of Brilliant Blue Toner for about 30 seconds until the background took on a distinct blue tone. After removing the remaining film, I washed and dried the print. Next,

I repeated the initial step of covering the print with frisket film, except that this time I removed the film to expose just the tulips and stems. In the final stages I used a soft-haired bush, cotton swabs, and colors from the Color Retouching Kit (some blended) to colorize the flowers and stems. The colors were diluted with water plus a drop or two of wetting agent to keep them uniform. I applied the colors in successive layers to reach the intensity I desired and then strengthened some areas with a brush and undiluted color.

Here was a more complicated attempt at hand coloring using a combination of artists' oil colors and dyes from the Berg Color Retouching and Hand Coloring Kit.

First, the staff in the girl's hand was painted with Yellow and the kimono with Green using a fairly large brush and undiluted dyes from the kit. Next, using low-tack frisket paper, the print was masked, and with a swivel knife I exposed the area (face and hands) to be treated with oils. The first color to go on was a flesh tone made from cadmium red medium and yellow ochre and blended smooth. I then worked in some orange, a touch of ultramarine blue in the shadow areas, and some vermillion for the lips and cheeks. All blending was done with cotton swabs and a finger tip. Finally, I removed the frisket mask and applied the background color with cotton balls in a very light coating, being careful not to encroach onto the colors already applied. The scarf was given a light tint of cadmium yellow. The hair was given a hint of raw umber and ultramarine blue. The white borders of the print were left masked until the last color was in place.

This photo reflects a combination of metallic toning and hand coloring. This print of traditional Japanese dolls was first given an overall toning bath in the Berg Brown/Copper toner. After the print was washed and dried I used a large sable brush and successive washes of Red-1 and Orange from the Color Retouching and Hand Coloring Kit for the dolls, and a smaller brush and Yellow and Green for the foreground leaves.

The intention here was to produce a soft watercolor effect by using diluted colors from the Berg Color Retouching and Hand Coloring Kit. In this case the paper, Kodak Ektalure paper with a lustre finish, is a warm-toned fiber-based paper that, when developed in a developer such as Selectol by Kodak, produces a very pleasing creamy tone. This paper also has a texture suited to the application of dyes or watercolors with a brush. I used a big, soft watercolor brush, and worked wet with diluted colors, sometimes blending with a cotton swab. The result is similar to that achieved by hand coloring with oils.

A pool of water draining from the air conditioning system had collected under the wheels of this jumbo jet parked at the ramp. A simple transformation using a brush and Red-1 from the Berg Color Retouching and Hand Coloring Kit made it appear as if this giant aircraft was giving up its very life blood.

This was what you might call a "free wheeling" experiment that had some unexpected but pleasing results. The subject was shot with backlighting coming from the sun streaming out of quickly moving clouds. I was a little disappointed in the image when I printed it until I decided to overexpose the foreground putting it almost in silhouette against the sky, which I held back by dodging.

Next I gave the print an overall soak in Berg Golden/Yellow toner for about five minutes. After rinsing the print and placing it flat on the back of a tray, I took a large soft brush and began to alternate Red-1 and Red-2 from the Color-Toning System,

laying on pools of color, and then moving the solution over the surface with the brush. I did this for about five minutes, periodically rinsing and wiping with a squeegee to check the progress. After the initial applications of color, I introduced a little of the Activator Solution, which I randomly applied with the brush as I had done with the color. I gave it another rinse, a wipe with a squeegee, and went back at it again with the Red-1 and Red-2 in selected spots. I doubt that I could duplicate the result exactly a second time.

The print was made on Ilford Multigrade II paper.

No careful blending or masking here. This is an example of unrestrained freehand hand coloring with the dyes from the Berg Color Retouching and Hand Coloring Kit. This time, however, the color was literally blobbed on with a large sable brush, and before the dye had a chance to dry it was moved around the surface of the print in a random fashion with the aid of the jet of air from an airbrush. An aerosol can of air probably would have worked just as well.

I used all but three or four of the colors from the kit, but could easily have included them all.

The print was made on Ilford Multigrade II paper.

diluted with water on the palette before you apply it to the print. (If you wish to protect the white print borders, first mask them out with low-tack frisket paper.) Lay the print on a flat surface, such as an inverted tray in a sink, and, with a cotton ball for large areas or a brush for finer work, apply the solution evenly, blotting up any excess with a dry cotton ball. By keeping the surface moist and working quickly, you can easily blend two or more adjacent colors, or, if you wish to keep the areas of color distinct, wait for each one to dry before adding the next. Remember that the dyes are transparent and that by laying one directly on top of another you change not only the density but the color tint as well.

For a bolder, hard-edged look, use an appropriate-sized brush and, working quickly to avoid showing any brush strokes, lay on the color straight from the bottle onto the dry print surface.

Always apply the retouching colors before any other materials, such as color retouching pencils or oils. If you like, you can finish off a hand-colored print with a spray of clear lacquer, either matte or glossy.

You can use the colors available in the Berg Color Retouching Kit for several other practical applications:

1. **Retouching "Red Eye".** The all-too-familiar "red eye" look is caused by the light reflected from the back of the eyeball when a flash is placed too close to the lens axis. It shows up in color photographs as an eerie red spot in the center of the pupil. This can be effectively retouched out by mixing one drop of Yellow to one drop of Blue-1 to make green, and then applying in diluted form as needed until the red is gone.

2. **Overall Correction.** Anyone who has done any amount of color printing will be familiar with the frustration of not getting quite the right filtration set in the enlarger colorhead and ending up with a print that is just slightly "off". With the high cost of color-print paper these days, one is understandably reluctant to make a second or third print. The Berg retouching colors can provide you with a simple, inexpensive answer to this common dilemma. Make up some varying dilutions of the three key colors used in color printing: cyan (Blue-1), magenta (Red-1), and Yellow. Begin with, say, five drops of each color to twenty ounces of water in separate containers. Now, with the aid of the Kodak Color Print Viewing Filters, determine the color correction that might be needed, dip the print into a bath of the appropriate color for a short time (one to five minutes), and then examine the results. Too much? Wash the print to remove the color or place it in a bath made up of one ounce of glacial acetic acid to one quart of water. For localized removal, blot (don't rub) with a cotton ball soaked in the same solution. Not enough color? Place the print back in the color bath for an additional time or increase the concentration of the color in the bath next time. When satisfied with the final result, rinse the print with water and hang it up to dry. This procedure can be used with equal effect with either color-negative prints such as Kodak Ektaflex prints, or Cibachrome prints. Color can be added to transparency material in the same way.

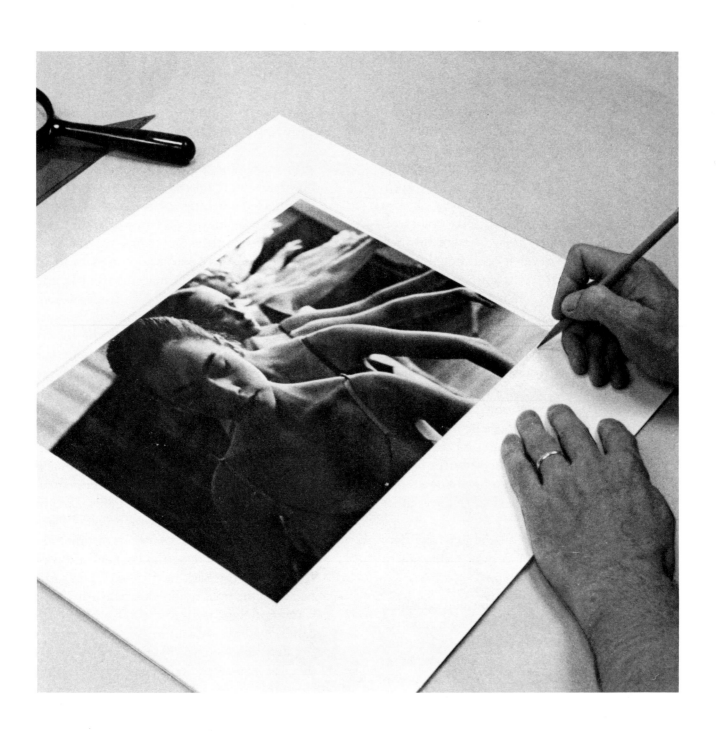

7

Archival Printing

Take a page of your daily newspaper, leave it out in the sun for a week or so and then bring it in and compare it with the newspaper you have just received. A noticeable difference, right? The exposed paper has probably yellowed and become brittle, and the type may have even faded somewhat. This is an extreme example of deterioration, nevertheless the lesson is clear: paper and, more importantly, photographic paper and the photographic image are vulnerable to some amount of breakdown unless steps are taken to protect them. Chemical reactions, ultraviolet radiation from the sun or artificial lighting, pollutants in the air, attacks by living microorganisms and changes in temperature and humidity are some of the factors that diminish the life of a photographic image. Manufacturers continually look for ways to enhance the durability of their photographic products, and though you will no doubt hear some dissenting voices, most photographers agree that we should make every effort to ensure that the images we produce will be as permanent as possible. In a nutshell this is what archival processing is all about.

The jury is still out on certain aspects of print permanence, particularly with regard to resin-coated papers, but there is general agreement on one thing: for *maximum* protection, black-and-white prints should be treated with a protective coating.

One of the oldest and most effective methods of treatment is chemical toning; another, the use

of a gold protective solution. Before we discuss them, however, let's look at some of the fundamentals of archival processing.

ARCHIVAL PROCESSING

Just as I have stressed the advantage of good housekeeping to minimize dust particles in the darkroom, it is important to realize that good darkroom technique is also essential as a guarantee against image deterioration. Keep utensils and containers scrupulously clean and avoid contaminating one chemical with another. If possible use separate containers and trays for each different chemical, and label them permanently. Glass containers are usually preferable to plastic or metal.

Washing, of course, plays a major role in removing residual chemicals, especially thiosulfate (fixer), which can be damaging to your print over the long term. The use of a fixer-removing product such as Berg Bath™, along with thorough and proper washing, is helpful in removing residual fixer.

Proper washing in itself is something more than swishing your print around in a water bath for a couple of minutes. The key to proper washing is to ensure that *fresh* water is circulated around the print, not only removing the imbedded chemicals from the paper, but flushing them away for good. There are two ways to accomplish this. One is to rotate your prints in a tray of running water with a siphon, periodically dumping the water and refilling to repeat the process. The other is to use a good archival print washer, which constantly circulates a fresh supply of water around the prints and which drains away the unwanted chemicals. Whichever method you use, you can check the effectiveness of your washing technique by testing the print with Kodak's Hypo Test Kit. Also, if you are concerned about the quality of water where you live, it's a good idea to install a filter in your water lines. Keep the wash water temperature between 65°F and 70°F (18°C and 22°C), and never less than 65°F (18°C) where very little washing benefit exists.

To this point the print is protected against internal contaminents, that is, chemicals imbedded in the paper. The next step is to protect it against external elements such as air pollutants and ultraviolet light. Before we do, however, a word about the permanence of some photographic materials.

Organic dyes, such as those used in color print photography, are susceptible to fading and lifetimes as short as a few years are not unusual, although recent research advances have produced more stable dyes. Retouching dyes, and the dyes in dye-toners are organic and should not be expected to have permanence beyond that of colors in color photographs. In archival terms, then, the less dye retouching done the better. To repeat, the emulsions on resin-coated papers have not proven to be very durable in the long term, and are not considered suitable for archival printing.

TONING FOR PROTECTION

Toning a fine print after it has been processed and washed is the final important step in ensuring maximum protection. In general, toners based on stable inorganic salts, such as the five Berg metallic toners, offer excellent protection and can actually extend the life of the image significantly. Selenium toning is an effective method of print protection as is gold treatment. Certain photo lacquers or sprays are said to possess protective properties against ultraviolet light, air pollutants, and other external image-destroying factors, but their effectiveness has not been proven.

SELENIUM TONING

Berg makes a Rapid Selenium Toner that many fine art printers use as a final archival step in the processing chain. The purpose of this technique is to convert the image silver into silver selenide, which is resistant to oxidation and contaminants. The procedure is carried out in full room light.

In addition to protecting the print from contaminants, selenium toning also changes the color of the print (the degree to which depends on the strength of the toner and the type of paper) from the usual greenish olive black to a warmer reddish black, and imparts a richness to the deep grays and blacks resulting in an overall improvement in contrast. The total effect can be very gratifying, especially if your print lacks that illusive intensity and depth.

Selenium toning is usually carried out after a two-bath fix and initial wash. Berg gives full instructions for using the toner with each bottle, but basically the procedure is to dilute the toner with water or Berg Bath™ (the dilution can vary considerably depending on the degree of toning you desire) and immerse the print in a tray of the solution for a period of about one to ten minutes, agitating intermittently. I find a dilution of 80 ounces of diluted Berg Bath™ to 6 ounces of Berg Selenium toner works well. As the toning progresses, it is helpful to compare the print being toned with an untoned print to help you judge when just the right amount of color shift and intensification has taken place.

In general, warm-toned papers show the most evidence of color change during toning and cold-toned papers show little or no change. Experiment with different papers and paper grades, and view your prints during toning under different light sources to see what variations in color and contrast are possible with this toner.

GOLD TREATMENT

Of all the methods used in the archival treatment of photographic images, gold protection has long been recognized as being the preeminent technique. The reason for this is quite fundamental. The metallic silver particles that make up the photographic image are, just as in the case of the family silverware, susceptible to tarnishing through oxidation. Gold, on the other hand, does not tarnish.

The Berg Gold Protective Solution is formulated to give a print an extremely thin covering layer of metallic gold, so thin in fact, that the yellow color of metallic gold is not observable. The product comes as a two-part solution that is mixed together with water at normal room temperature. In full room light the prewashed prints are immersed into the mixed solution for approximately ten to fifteen minutes. Master printers will tell you that gold coating adds a certain "snap" and depth to prints and may, in the case of warm-toned paper, produce a very subtle shift to a cooler tone. Cold-toned papers are not likely to show any change in tone.

As you might expect, this method of protection is relatively expensive. It is only used on black-and-white prints.

8

The Final Steps: Drying, Storing, Mounting and Framing

DRYING
THE PRINT

When the photographic print has been passed through the processing chain, and then either toned or treated in some way, it should be given a final wash and air dried. Any major corrective measures such as chemical reducing should be carried out now, but spotting or minor retouching can be done even after the print is mounted.

Air drying at room temperature or in a warm air print drier is preferable to using blotters, which sometime contain harmful chemicals and fibers that stick to the emulsion. Some photographers suspend their prints from a line with plastic clothes pegs; the preferred way is to lay your prints emulsion down on wooden frames covered with fiberglass or plastic screening, the materials for which you can buy at most hardware stores. The humidity of the air in the drying room has a great deal to do with print curling, and there is little you can do to avoid it. Resin-coated papers present little problem with curling during drying, but with fiber-based papers after air drying I slip them into a dry-mount press at

the lowest heat level for twenty seconds or so to flatten them before mounting or storing.

STORAGE

For short-term storage, the empty boxes in which you received your printing paper will serve well, but for the very long term you would be well advised to invest in some archival boxes made from acid-free board. Store your prints in a cool, dark place in low humidity.

Avoid writing on the back of your prints with anything other than a lead pencil applied lightly in the edge area, as many ordinary inks can, over the long period, leach through to the image side. The retouching pencil mentioned in chapter 5 is useful for writing information on the back of resin-coated paper.

MOUNTING

As a general rule, avoid the use of any of the ordinary household glues for mounting your prints unless the glue is a type of flour or rice starch paste used by framers for mounting art prints. Certain spray mounting glues made especially for photographs are generally safe to use, and you should follow the manufacturers' recommendations.

By far the most practical and easiest mounting method is dry-mounting. Dry-mount hot presses are relatively expensive, but are worth the investment if you intend to do any amount of print mounting. Also, some do-it-yourself framing shops carry this equipment for you to use. When you use this type of press, or a hot tacking iron to fix the print to the board, use the lowest heat recommended for the minimum time required. Instructions usually come with the tissue and the mounting press. Specifically, never use excess heat for prolonged times with toned prints, and do not use a dry-mount press for prints that have been hand colored with oils.

Prints should only be mounted on what is commonly called "rag board", meaning, roughly, that there is no wood pulp used in its manufacture. The rag board should also be designated acid free, or pH neutral, which means that it is free of sulphurous contaminants. Consult a good framer, graphic arts supplier or photo dealer for the best variety of mounting boards to use, and be prepared to pay more for the better types. If you have spent a considerable amount of time and taken great care to produce an archival photographic print there seems little economy to be gained by mounting it with inferior materials. If you want your great-grandchildren to enjoy your print in close to its original condition, then use the best materials you can find.

For methods and techniques on cutting mats and mounting procedures consult a good book on framing at your local library or crafts shop. *Caring for Photographs* by Time Life Books and *The Print* by Ansel Adams both contain very useful and informative chapters on the subject.

SPRAYING
Periodically throughout this manual I have mentioned the use of photo sprays. On the one hand, lacquer sprays probably do provide some degree of protection, certainly against fingerprints and dust, and they have added advantages in that they tend to enrich the blacks and improve the color saturation in toned or tinted photographs. There are a number of these lacquers available in aerosol cans designated glossy or matte. On the other hand, a properly processed and toned art print for display should require no protection beyond proper mounting and framing.

FRAMING
The selection of mat and frame is too much of an individual consideration to make anything but the most general recommendations. A simple neutral white mat is invariably the best choice for display prints, and I would caution against trying to "match" the dominant color of a print with a corresponding colored mat. Don't overstate. Also, if you decide to sign your print, use a light touch with a hard pencil, preferably on the mat surface on the right side just below the edge of the mounted print. You may include the date next to the signature, and if you feel you must give your print a title (does it really need one?) then write it on the left side in line with your signature.

Metal frames, an economical choice, can be purchased precut in various sizes and come in a good selection of colors and finishes. Certain types have simple snap-in backing, which makes it very easy to change the photograph later on.

Glass also comes precut in standard sizes and in two types, clear and nonglare. I have a very strong personal bias towards the clear type for photographs, because I don't like the built-in haze of the so-called nonglare glass, which robs the print of its inherent richness.

To sum up, the whole point of mounting and framing for display, whether in home or gallery, is to lend dignity to the print without drawing attention away from the photographic image. Aim for simplicity and quality in your materials and your viewers will be grateful.

9

Recording the Data

One of the most intriguing aspects of manipulating a black-and-white print after it has gone through the normal processing chain is that often the results gained are unique and unexpected. There will be times when you will want to duplicate as closely as possible a certain intensity of toning, or some special effect on a subsequent print. To achieve this sort of consistency you will need some method of recording the exact sequence of steps and the dilutions, times, and methods that were used to produce a certain result.

I've worked out a system of my own, and some forms created on a computer with a graphics program. You are welcome to copy these, or use them as a guide to make up your own. However you decide to record the data, it's a good idea to make your notations immediately after each step of the procedure in a book or file kept just for this purpose.

A simple loose-leaf binder containing forms used for recording, processing, and toning data is a handy thing to keep close at hand in the darkroom. The forms serve as a means of recording for later reference not only any particularly good result or special effect obtained but also information about the dismal failures and comments on how to avoid similar pitfalls in future attempts.

Detailed data recording may seem like a lot of trouble to some, and you may be quite content to simply make a few shorthand notes on the back of your print. Fair enough. On the other hand, the following forms are designed to be convenient, step-by-step check lists for recording as much or as little data as you care to, in just about any printing situation. I have indicated how I would use the forms to record the information pertaining to the photo illustration on page 14.

Following are specific instructions for the use of the *Printing Data Sheet*.

1. Use your own shorthand or symbols (e.g., for moderately heavy burning I use "+ +").

2. Include as much or as little information as you care to.

3. Under the processing section, I have no record of the use of an "acid stop bath" because it is a consistently standard procedure and need not be included. (The acid stop bath would normally follow the developer.)

4. This form serves well for most prints with simple or no toning/retouching. For complicated toning/retouching use this form and the *Toning Data Sheet*.

PRINTING DATA SHEET _____

EXPOSURE		FILM TYPE		FILM SIZE		DATE	
		ASA/ISO	E.I.	FILE NO.		FRAME	
		SUBJECT		TITLE			
		LOCATION		JOB			
		REMARKS					

PRINTING	Paper Type and Grade	Paper Size	Image Size	Filter No.	Lens	f Stop	Time	Enl. Ht.
PRINT 1								
Dodge								
Burn								
Other								

PRINTING	Paper Type and Grade	Paper Size	Image Size	Filter No.	Lens	f Stop	Time	Enl. Ht.
PRINT 2								
Dodge								
Burn								
Other								

PROCESSING	Remarks				
	Developer 1		Dilution	Time	
PRINT 1	Developer 2		Dilution	Time	
Fix 1	Time	Wash	Hypo Elim.	Time	
Fix 2	Time	Wash	Hypo Elim.	Time	
Remarks					

PROCESSING	Remarks				
	Developer 1		Dilution	Time	
PRINT 2	Developer 2		Dilution	Time	
Fix 1	Time	Wash	Hypo Elim.	Time	
Fix 2	Time	Wash	Hypo Elim.	Time	
Remarks					

TONE/RETOUCH	Remarks
PRINT 1	

TONE/RETOUCH	Remarks
PRINT 2	

PRINTING DATA SHEET _12_

EXPOSURE		FILM TYPE _Tri-X prof._		FILM SIZE _120_		DATE _June 86_
		ASA/ISO _400_	E.I. _400_	FILE NO. _10-86_		FRAME _2_
		SUBJECT _Bodybuilder_			TITLE _—_	
		LOCATION _—_			JOB _—_	
		REMARKS _Self assignment_				

PRINTING	Paper Type and Grade	Paper Size	Image Size	Filter No.	Lens	f Stop	Time	Enl. Ht.
PRINT 1	_Seagull 3_	_11 x 14_	_10 X 11_	_—_	_75_	_11_	_10_	_9¼_
Dodge	_Below chest (−)_							
Burn	_Hands and forearms (++)_							
Other								

PRINTING	Paper Type and Grade	Paper Size	Image Size	Filter No.	Lens	f Stop	Time	Enl. Ht.
PRINT 2	_Ilford MG II_	_8 x 10_	_6¾ x 8¾_	_3_	_75_	_11_	_6_	_7_
Dodge								
Burn								
Other								

PROCESSING	Remarks _Grade 3 Seagull too hard . . ._			
	Developer 1 _Selectol-soft_		Dilution _1:2_	Time _45 s_
PRINT 1	Developer 2 _Dektol_		Dilution _1:2_	Time _1:30_
Fix 1 _Kodak_	Time _3_	Wash	Hypo Elim.	Time
Fix 2 _✓_	Time _3_	Wash _1 hr._	Hypo Elim.	Time
Remarks				

PROCESSING	Remarks			
	Developer 1 _Multigrade_		Dilution _1:9_	Time _1 min._
PRINT 2	Developer 2		Dilution	Time
Fix 1 _Ilfofix_	Time _30_	Wash _2 min_	Hypo Elim.	Time
Fix 2	Time	Wash	Hypo Elim.	Time
Remarks				

TONE/RETOUCH	Remarks _Kodak selenium toner for 15 mins. Dilution:_
	80 ozs. hypo clearing agent to 6 ozs sel. toner.
PRINT 1	

TONE/RETOUCH	Remarks _Berg brown/copper toner for 1 min at stock_
	strength.
PRINT 2	

TONING DATA SHEET _____

PRINT	Print Data Sheet No.		File No.		Frame
	Subject				

Remarks

TONING	Remarks

STEP	TONER/TINT	DILUTION	TIME	WASH	REDEV	TIME	OTHER

RETOUCHING	Remarks

TONING DATA SHEET

PRINT	Print Data Sheet No. 7	File No. 26-84	Frame 13A
	Subject W.W.1 Flyer		

Remarks	Copied photo from family album on FP4 film.
	Print on Portriga Rapid 3, matte,
	Dodge out background with oval mask.

TONING	Remarks Bleach out damaged area with
	ferricyanide. Fix and wash.

STEP	TONER/TINT	DILUTION	TIME	WASH	REDEV	TIME	OTHER
A.	Brown / copper						
	toner	stock	3-5 mins	10 mins			
	— or —						
B	RC sepia toner						
	1. Bleach	stock	1½ mins	10 mins			
	2. Toner	✓	2 mins	45 mins			

RETOUCHING	Remarks
	1. Spotting and corrections with warm black
	2. Try for detail in face/head
	3. Berg retouch colours: orange/brown
	orange
	yellow
	green

——Appendix——

Manufacturers and Products_____

Following is a list of manufacturers and some specialty products that have been mentioned in this book and which fall outside the usual materials you might expect to find in an average photo supply store. The list is by no means complete. The Berg line of products is also listed and can be purchased from most photo supply retailers. Information regarding the characteristics and properties of various photographic papers and processing chemistry can be obtained by consulting a knowledgeable salesperson at your photo dealer. In most cases, your personal preferences will determine the final choice.

Berg Color-Tone Inc.
72 Ward Road,
Lancaster, New York
14086
Telephone (716) 681-2696
Fax (716) 684-0511

PRODUCTS:
Berg Bath™ (Hypo Eliminator
  /Washing Aid After Toning)
Berg Weekender® Toning Kit
Brilliant Blue Toning Solution
Brown/Copper Toning Solution
Color Retouching and Hand Coloring Kit
Color-Toning System
Dehardening Solution
Gold Protective Solution
Golden/Yellow Toning Solution
Selenium Toning Solution
RC Sepia Toning Solution
Touchrite® Brush Kit
Touchrite® Kit

Bogen Photo
565 East Crescent Ave.
P.O. Box 506
Ramsey, New Jersey
07446-0506
PRODUCTS:
Dry Mount Presses

Seal Products Inc.
550 Spring Street
Naugatuck, Connecticut
06770
PRODUCTS:
Dry Mount Tissue
Dry Mount Presses

Ulano Corporation
255 Butler Street
Brooklyn, New York
11217
PRODUCTS:
Swivel Knives

Index⎯⎯⎯⎯⎯⎯⎯⎯⎯⎯